WINDOWS TO
EXPERIENCE

POCKET EDITION

Published from
Mardukite Borsippa HQ, San Luis Valley, Colorado
Mardukite Academy & Systemology Society
for spiritual or educational purposes only

WINDOWS TO EXPERIENCE

THE FILTERS OF HUMAN PERCEPTION

A Basic Course developed
by Joshua Free
for the Systemology Society

© 2023, JOSHUA FREE

ISBN : 978-1-961509-20-7

Also available in hardcover as
"Fundamentals of Systemology"

Pocket Paperback Edition — *October 2023*

mardukite.com

SYSTEMOLOGY is the
"New Thought" of the 21st Century.

It is the study of how
Spiritual Beings with unlimited power
became entrapped in the
Human Condition.

This study is an applied philosophy
— "A Pathway to Ascension" —
that charts our way back out,
freeing the True Self to experience
higher levels of existence again.

Systemology is the true science of the
"Matrix."

After more than a decade of
development, the "Fundamentals of
Systemology" are concisely explored
here in the first official
"Basic Course" on the subject ever
given by Joshua Free for the
Mardukite Academy.

It's time to discover
who you really are...
because you
were never "Human."

Fundamentals of Systemology
Basic Course Lesson Booklets

Lesson #1
BEING MORE THAN HUMAN
Rediscovering the Spiritual Self

Lesson #2
REALITIES IN AGREEMENT
Spiritual Life and The Universe

Lesson #3
WINDOWS TO EXPERIENCE
The Filters of Human Perception

Lesson #4
ANCIENT SYSTEMOLOGY
Wisdom From the Arcane Tablets

Lesson #5
A HISTORY OF SYSTEMOLOGY
Evolution of a Spiritual Science

Lesson #6
SYSTEMOLOGY PROCESSING
Practices of Spiritual Awakening

TABLET OF CONTENTS

"BASIC COURSE" INTRODUCTION

LESSON THREE:
WINDOWS OF EXPERIENCE—
THE FILTERS OF HUMAN PERCEPTION

APPENDIX

INTRODUCTION
TO THE
"BASIC COURSE"

WELCOME, SEEKER!
YOUR JOURNEY ON THE PATHWAY
BEGINS HERE

This is a basic course in *Systemology*—
specifically, the fundamental principles of
Mardukite Systemology.

Quite simply: *Mardukite Systemology* is a
new evolution in Human understanding
about the "systems" governing *Spiritual
Life*, *Reality*, the *Universe* and all *Existences*.

In many ways, *Systemology* is a 21st Century breakthrough that continues the leg-
acy—and unifies the original pursuits—
of early 20th Century "*American New
Thought*" and other metaphysical schools
of philosophy and mysticism. These are
mostly all generalized (and often dis-
missed) in modern culture as "*New Age*"
beliefs, though they are actually quite

"*old*" —some even based on the most ancient known writings of discovered civilizations.

Mardukite Systemology was once concisely described as "an applied spiritual technology of the 21st Century A.D., based on spiritual wisdom from the 21st Century B.C." because of our use of "*Mesopotamian*" *Arcane Tablets* as source material for its foundations (and from which it retains a "*Mardukite*" designation).

The original *New Thought Movement* in America applied a "Western Civilization" approach to "Eastern" concepts—concepts that we now take for granted today, but of which were relatively unknown to the general population at that time. The movement sought to develop an "applied spiritual philosophy" whereby an individual could unlock their hidden potentials, untapped "*Knowingness*" and higher spiritual states of *Beingness*. These innate or native conditions of *Self* (as a *Spirit*) are blocked—or "fragmented"—by a "human" preoccupation with identifying *Self* as one and the same with the material body that it is merely using as a "vehicle" to experience (communicate and interact) within *this* Physical Universe.

Early *New Thought* work primarily emphasized practical "healing" applications (*mental healing, faith healing, &tc.*)—but at its very core, we may restate the ultimate pursuit or original focus was to "free humans *to be* their ideal native spiritual state."

This goal has been with us—lingering on the periphery of the "surface world"—for much longer than the existence of a *New Thought Movement*. In fact, for as long as "spiritual beings" have found themselves entrapped by a "Human Condition" and enforced to experience *this* "material existence" (fragmented from their true *Self*),

13

a continuing pursuit has ensued to correct the situation—at least by those individuals still retaining enough *Awareness* to realize it.

Humans have been figuring on how to break free from the *"Matrix"* for a very long time. The desire or ambition to rise above the "standard-issue" Human Condition is already there. But the truth is that many other remotely similar "evolutions" of *New Thought* have dissolved into "multi-level marketing" schemes, "motivational pop-psychology" coaching, abusive "cult-like" movements—or heavily promoted books that skyrocket to the peaks of literary "bestseller lists" only to be discarded soon after and forgotten. They all share one thing in common: they all seem to capitalize on an innate desire or yearning we have to *"ascend"*—but, of course, without delivering stable results.

Even the most pious and well-meaning

philosophies and spiritual sciences have each fallen short of piercing the *"invisible barriers"* of perception separating *this* "Physical Universe" from any other "higher" existence—and with it, blocking our "way out" and the *Awareness* of our own true native state as an *Eternal Spirit.*

SYSTEMOLOGY:
21ST CENTURY NEW THOUGHT

Our *Systemology* is a new approach to *"Self-Actualization"*—completely relevant for the modern age and the future—and quite different from previous attempts or other traditions you might find.

Former attempts at overcoming *"barriers"* or *"gates"* of *reality* have included simply pretending that they don't exist, rejecting all material existence—all *time* and *space* —as an *"illusion"* and consequently losing the ability to actually *confront* the *reality* of anything *"As-It-Is."*

Our *Systemology* is also the answer to the "great mysteries" pervading the material sciences and natural philosophies; for they only seek to further qualify and validate the *reality agreements* made for *this* Physical Universe—and thus their level of understanding can never successfully pass the "barriers" either.

When applying our philosophy and techniques, the "systematic routes" outlined for an individual to increase their *"Actualized Awareness"* (and reach gradually higher toward their *"Spiritual Ascension"*) is referred to as *"The Pathway"*—and we call that individual a *"Seeker."*

At the start of *The Pathway*, early *routes* emphasize establishing a strong personal foundation of emotional well-being and mental strength before a *Seeker* is introduced to more advanced exercises and practices.

As a *Seeker* increases their *Awareness* in this lifetime, their spiritual "*Knowingness*" also increases—which is to say their sense of "*certainty*"; a certainty on *Life*, on this and other *Universes*, but more accurately, an increased certainty on *Self* as a practically unlimited "spiritual being" *having* an enforced restrictive "human experience."

One of the goals of "*Systematic Processing*" techniques in *Systemology* is to increase the ability of a *Seeker* to actually control and direct the "*attention*" of *Self* as a "spiritual being"—and as a result, *knowingly* increase command of the "human experience." This is a part of what we mean by "*Actualized Awareness*."

THREE STATES OF KNOWINGNESS

Raising a *Seeker's* level of *Actualized Awareness* requires, by definition, "bringing what is *hidden* (or not consciously known) up into the realm of *light* or *Knowingness*." We might go as far to say, as an imperfect example, that there are three primary states of *Knowingness*: *actual knowing*, *almost knowing* and *not-knowing*.

Actual knowing is what an individual is conscious of and can easily recall as needed. It makes up our "surface" (or "above-the-surface") thoughts; what is *"actually known"* and available to *Self* for "inspection" or analytical thought. This includes what we have *certainty* on as part of our *reality*.

Then, there are other *things* "below-the-

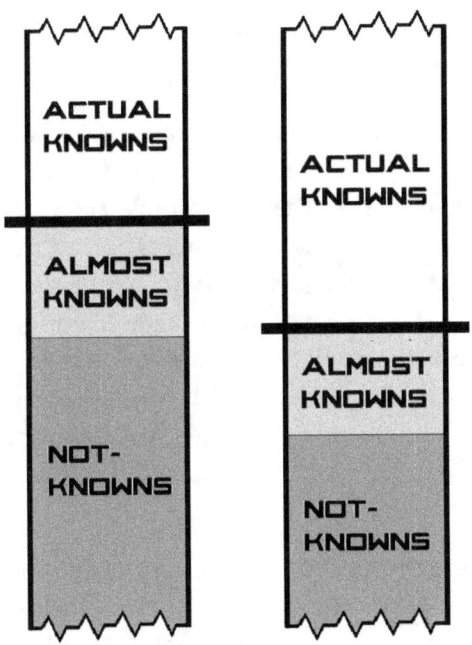

surface" that we do not easily remember (or have any *reality* on)—and these fit our other categories of *almost knowing* and *not-knowing*. The difference between these other two states is how *far* "below-the-surface" a *thing* is.

What you *"almost know"* are those *things* just "below-the-surface"—so *close* to the "surface" that they are almost accessible. This "gray area" includes what an individual is *uncertain* of. With a little assistance (*"Systematic Processing"* techniques), you can actually move a *thing* that is *"almost known"* to an "above-the-surface" state of *"actually knowing"* or remembering again. Only then may it be treated with any *certainty*.

There are also memories very deeply buried "below-the-surface." This includes suppressed data that is not currently accessible—and therefore, presently *"not-known."* Once again, there is a way to move *things* from this state into another state. For this to happen, the previous *"almost known" things* ("just-below-the-surface") need to be "purged" (at least partially) by *"resurfacing"* them into *"actually known" things*.

As more layers of *"almost knowns"* are *resurfaced* into *"actual knowns,"* more of what is *"not-known"* becomes accessible within the "gray area." *Systematic Processing* techniques of *Systemology* are intended to target this "gray area"— promoting increased *realizations* by elevating more knowledge to a state of *Actual Awareness*.

HOW TO STUDY
A SYSTEMOLOGY COURSE

Most *Seekers* study and practice *Systemology* at-a-distance and independent of the

"Mardukite Academy" or any "Master-level" mentors trained therein. This means that the *books* (and to a lesser degree, the *internet*) are the only means of direct contact a *Seeker* maintains with the "Systemology Society" during their studies.

It is quite common to have had negative past experiences with "education" and "learning"—whether in school or other type of instruction. This can sometimes inhibit an individual from pursuing a new *study* later on in their lifetime. However, simply following a few guidelines, ensures a *Seeker's* successful and positive experience when studying this course book—and, of course, the subject of *Systemology* as a whole.

To effectively study and understand a new subject (or a higher gradient of a subject), an individual must be "interested" in the material. A *Seeker* chooses to study *Systemology* because they "want" to, which is to say, on their own "*Self-Determinism.*" While modern society likes to enforce "agreement" (to further solidify a *reality*), a genuine "interest" and true "understanding" can only occur on one's own *Self-Determinism.*

Having established interest, the next *barrier* to understanding is "vocabulary" (words) and "semantics" (meaning). Any specific study, science or tradition is distinguished by the *words* used to communicate it. For true communication to occur, the intended "meaning" for each "word" used must be clearly defined and perfectly understood by the reader or receiver. We call this *"A-for-A"* or *"one-to-one"* communication.

Misunderstood words are the most common reason an individual abandons studying a subject. To relay a proper communication of *Systemology* concepts to a *Seeker*, we use very specific language in our course books. There are newer concepts that more obviously require defining when introduced; and some of our terminology uses familiar words, but with a different or specific meaning than when used elsewhere.

When a misunderstanding occurs, *Awareness* declines. These generally begin to "stack up" after the first occurrence and the level of interest and attention will also decline. This is how a "confusion" develops and the individual will get "bored" with the subject, feel tired, and unable to concentrate.

In extreme cases of confusion, there will be no future interest in studying or "looking at" something further. Feelings of "anger" and "sadness" may result (because one had originally *intended* on knowing something), followed by lower-level opposing "considerations" such as:

"didn't really want to know" or "it probably isn't very good anyways."

The misunderstood word that an individual passed in their study may not be immediately obvious. One solution is to return to the part of the material that was still interesting and enjoyable to read. When scanning around that area of text, there is likely to be a new word (or specific use of a familiar word) that is unclear, but was passed by unnoticed. All *Systemology* books include their own *glossary*. Using this *glossary* and a high-quality dictionary will help resolve this misunderstanding once it is located.

With "interest" and "understanding" secure, the next challenge of learning concerns making a subject *"tangible"*—which means handling it as a *"some-thing"* in the individual's personal *reality* or *Universe*.

Studying intellectual or "philosophical" subjects from a *book* requires excessive amounts of *"thought creation"* — of handling many conceptual images and ideas *"imagined"* solidly in one's "mind" in order to actually "look at" what one is studying. These also require a certain amount of present-time *attention* or *Awareness* to sustain a continual *creation*.

When an individual lacks "objective" examples (objects, graphic representations or direct experience) to examine, they may become "overwhelmed" by "mental-mass" if maintaining too many of their own *images*. This prompts feelings of being "worn out" or "weighed down" — and *considerations* that one "must take a break" or that the subject is "too difficult."

The obvious remedy is to supplement "book-learning" with objective or physical examples. Rather than simply studying or memorizing a series of "dry facts" from an "outside source" (and then returning to "ordinary" life), a student that does understand the material will take it up as their "own" *viewpoint*.

By taking the philosophies up as one's "own" *viewpoint*, the materially is effectively "owned" by the individual. They are not *looking* through a *lens* of someone else. The *"responsibility"* taken by this *ownership* means the freedom to apply information to everyday life and determine the truth of a matter for one's *Self*.

The final *barrier* to learning is the *knowledge* (or "know-*ledge*") itself—the *ledge* or *level* from which a person *knows* or *understands*. A "basic fact" could have many *levels* of potential understanding. To interpret *reality*, an individual "stands" on the *ledge-level* (or *gradient*) of *Knowingness* they have the most "certainty" on.

An effective education of any subject is

taught on a *gradient*. This is what is intended by introducing the study of something in "*grades*." Rather than treating a subject as one total mass, true learning is achieved by increasing one's understanding on a *gradual* incline upward. The *ascent* to a mountaintop is not successfully achieved in one leap, but by targeting and reaching specific checkpoints along the way.

In 2019, the "*Grades*" were established for the "Mardukite Academy" to properly indicate what level of understanding a specific book or course is intended for. The entry-point to directly study materials of the Systemology Society at the Academy is "*Grade-III*." Lower *grades* pertain to other *Mardukite* subjects treated separately from Systemology. Higher *grades* continue to explore the "theories and practices" of the Systemology Society as a complete "*Pathway to Ascension*."

This *Basic Course* consists of a series of lessons (booklets) that teach the *"Fundamentals of Systemology."* It is an appropriate entry-point for a new *Systemology* student. It is also applicable to more advanced *Seekers* wanting to increase their *certainty* of understanding at higher *grades* as well.

To study *Systemology* just like a student at the Academy: a *Seeker* reads through all instructional material in a *Basic Course* lesson (booklet) and then performs any practical exercises indicated at the end. Before continuing on to the next lesson (booklet), the material is read again and the light exercises are reapplied.

The second pass through the material is likely to result in different *"realizations"* (an increased *level of understanding*) than the first time. Exercises may seem more vivid or significant. *Seekers* should feel cheerful and confident in their *understan-*

ding of a section (or lesson) before proceeding even further on *The Pathway*.

YOUR FIRST STEPS ON THE PATHWAY

Systemology is a "holistic" approach to understanding the human experience. It is not actually a singular "subject" in itself, but rather, a way to "view" the many "subjects" of *Life* and all *Existence*. Its "scope" is not restricted to the rigidly fixed *considerations* of any one "subject" exclusively. Yet, for us to properly communicate its specific intended meaning, *Systemology* does require its own unique basic vocabulary.

The "basic vocabulary" and "*Fundamentals*" of *Systemology* are studied together early on *The Pathway*. They are consistent for the remaining upper-*grades*. It is our *understanding* of them that evolves as we progress.

The entire structure of *Systemology* rests on foundations of earlier material and earlier researches—such as those found in the earlier *grades* of Mardukite Academy. However, in 2019, new developments made it possible for a *Seeker* to start upon *The Pathway* without first spending years navigating around the pitfalls of other avenues and earlier *grade* subjects. As an extension of the original Academy, the Systemology Society continues to map and define the upper-*grade routes* of our philosophy.

The *Fundamentals of Systemology* are explored throughout the *Basic Course*. The critical foundations of its vocabulary and concepts (from *Grade-II*) were concisely collected in 2019 as an essay—"*Mardukite Zuism: A Brief Introduction*." It is summarized below to provide a more complete introduction to the "lessons" of the *Basic Course*. Each "lesson" will go on to examine this data in greater detail.

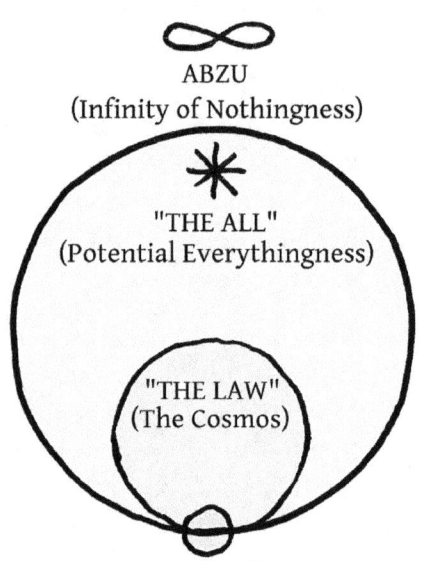

ABZU
(Infinity of Nothingness)

"THE ALL"
(Potential Everythingness)

"THE LAW"
(The Cosmos)

FOUNDATIONS OF SYSTEMOLOGY

Mardukite Zuism is a precursor to *Systemology.* It concerns an intensive archaeological study into the *Arcane Tablets* of Ancient Mesopotamia. Such tablet writings were once used to systematize an understanding of all cosmic knowledge— and they include the Babylonian *Epic of Creation.*

The *Epic of Creation* describes *ALL* ("ANKI") as separated into two *existences*: "AN" and "KI"—literally "heaven" and "earth"—which is to say *"spiritual"* ("AN") and *"physical"* ("KI"). Exterior to, and beyond, the *"potential everythingness"* of all *spiritual* existence and *physical* existence is only an Infinity of Nothingness ("ABZU").

In *Systemology*, we refer to the same two separate states of existence as *"Alpha"*

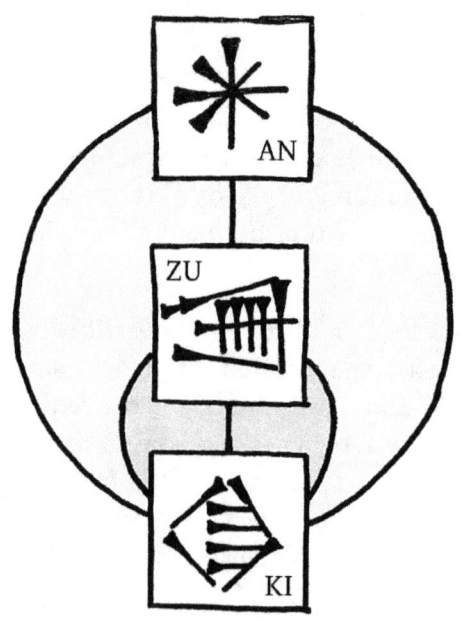

(*spiritual*) and "*Beta*" (*physical*). They are connected only by "*Spiritual Life Awareness*" or "ZU"—a term we have retained in *Systemology* (and for which *Mardukite Zuism* is named). Therefore, we have "*spiritual systems*" and "*physical systems*" connected by "ZU."

The "*Alpha*" *Universe*—of "metaphysical" or "spiritual" energy-matter—is not dependent on the "*Beta*" *Universe* to exist. The two exist independent of one another, except for a single channel or conduit maintaining a connection, which *is* the *Awareness* (the *Spiritual Life-Energy* or "ZU") of an "*Alpha-Spirit*."

"ZU" originates from an "*Alpha*" (*spiritual*) state, separate and distinct from the conditions of "*Beta*" existence that we experience as the *Physical Universe*. "ZU" is *Awareness*—the *Life-Force* or *Thought-Power* that "acts" or "impinges" on an "organism" in *Beta-Existence*.

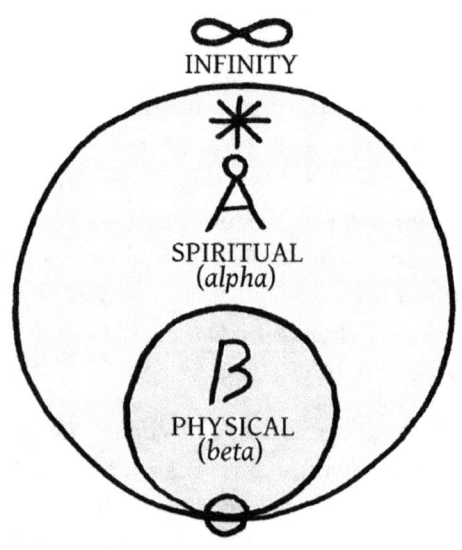

INFINITY

SPIRITUAL
(*alpha*)

PHYSICAL
(*beta*)

For example: the "intention" to read this book, or "commanding" a body to turn a page—those specific components are not actually a part of *this* existence. They are manifestations of a *Spiritual Awareness* (*Alpha*) acting upon an "organic body" (*Beta*). The *"Alpha-Spirit"* is the actual "Eternal" *Self*, which perceives and engages with *Beta-Existence* (*e.g.*, "Life on Earth") by using a "temporary" organic body or *"genetic vehicle."*

The *Alpha-Spirit* engages a *"ZU-Line"*—a *spiritual* "life-line" of *Attention* and *Awareness* ("ZU") energy—to an "organic body" or *genetic-vehicle* in order to directly experience a *"physical"* *Beta-Existence.*

We use the term *"Self-Honesty"* in *Systemology* to describe the original native *"Alpha"* state of true *Self-Directed* "Beingness" and crystal clear *"Knowingness."* *Self-Honesty* is the most basic "personality" or

37

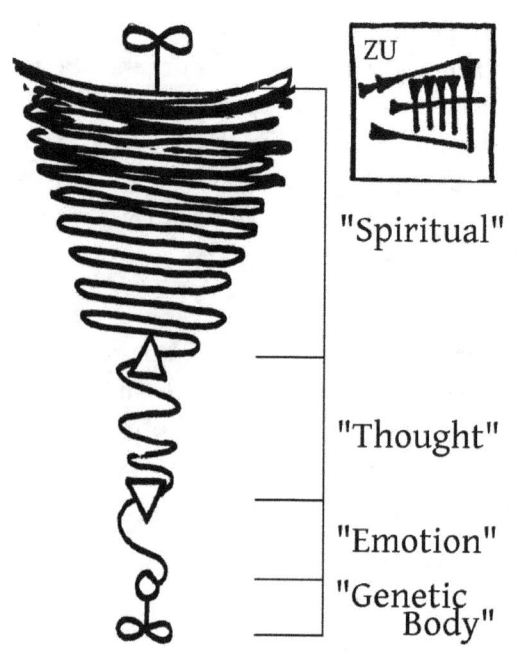

ZU

"Spiritual"

"Thought"

"Emotion"

"Genetic
Body"

true expression of *Self* (*Alpha-Spirit*) as *"I-AM"*—a *Self-Determined* state that is *free* of artificial attachments, automatic reaction-response mechanisms, or enforced (*other-determined*) *"reality-agreements"* concerning the Human Condition.

Applying philosophic routes and systematic methods of *Systemology* in order to return *Awareness* of *Self* to its true *"Source"* is referred to as *"The Pathway."* Its structure is based on archaic "models" from the "Ancient Near East" (*Mesopotamia, &tc.*) and elsewhere—such as the *"Chakras,"* the Babylonian *"Ladder of Lights"* (*Star-Gates*), and several versions of *"Kabbalah."*

For example: the Mesopotamians built "stepped-pyramids" as temples—called *"ziggurats"*—serving to remind us of the "ZU" bridging the *spiritual* and *physical* systems. Babylonians constructed *ziggurats* to correspond with *seven* primary "steps" or *"Gates."*

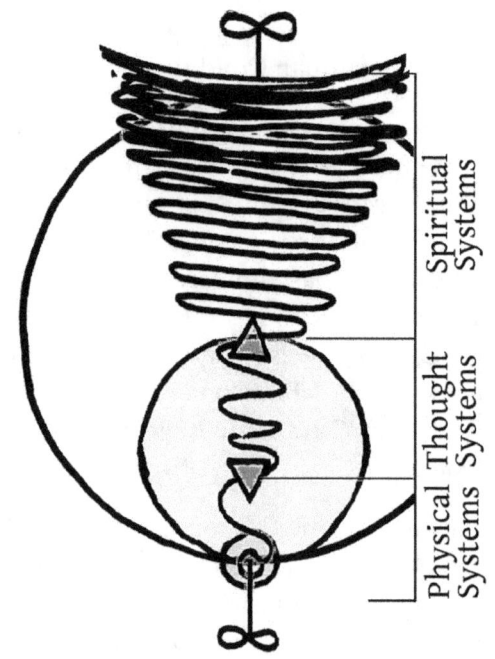

Spiritual Systems

Physical Thought Systems Systems

The "gradients" or "tiers" of the Babylonian *Ladder of Lights* represent *The Pathway*, because they define the *levels* of *Actualized Awareness* (and *Self-Honesty*)—the states of *Self-purification*—between the "standard-issue" *Human Condition* and *Infinity*. This is the *route* we travel for our *"spiritual defragmentation"* or *Ascension*.

BASIC VOCABULARY REVIEW PUZZLE

ACROSS

3. The standard-issue default manner of filtering perceptions of the Universe, as Self is experiencing it. (*2 words*)

4. The condition of being misaligned, broken apart, shattered, fractured, distorted, or otherwise separated into parts, compared to its original state.

7. A student or practitioner studying and applying Systemology philosophy.

8. The True Self or I-AM Awareness. (*2 words, hyphenated*)

10. The nature of the Physical Universe or material existence.

11. Another way to say "the agreement about what something is."

DOWN

1. The physical body, or any organic life, may serve as your ___. (*2 words*)

2. Regimen or routine of Systemology practices, techniques or exercises that increase Actualized Awareness of Self.

5. Returning to the original native state (or Source of the Spiritual Self) is known universally as ____.

6. A stream of energy connecting Spiritual Awareness to physical existence. (*2 words, hyphenated*)

9. The progressive journey taken in Systemology is referred to as "*The* ___."

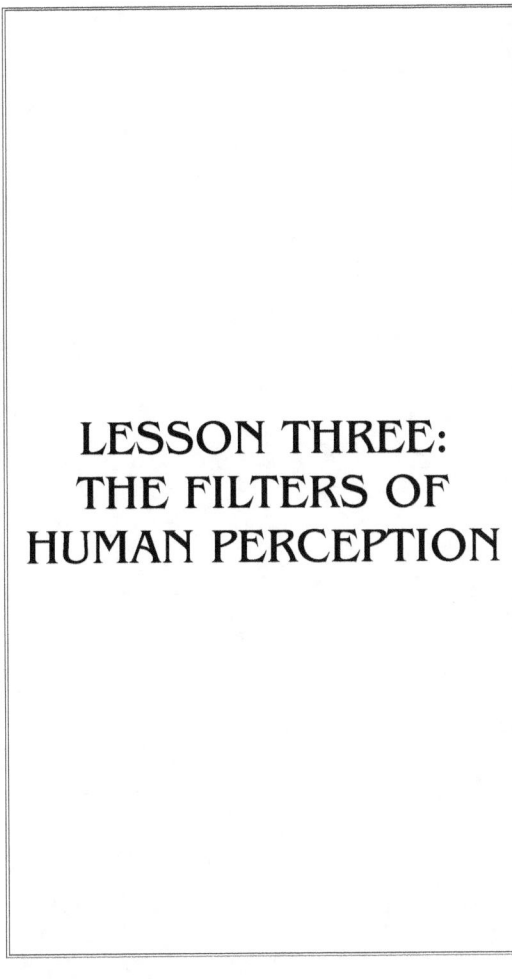

LESSON THREE:
THE FILTERS OF
HUMAN PERCEPTION

LESSON THREE
THE FILTERS OF HUMAN
PERCEPTION

"If the doors of perception were cleansed,
every thing would appear to man as it is,
Infinite.
For man has closed himself up,
until he sees all things
through narrow chinks of his cavern."
—William Blake (1793)

Many individuals are likely to define *"perception"* and *"Awareness"* as the same —and they *are* quite similar. The basic range of "Human Perception" is charted on the *"Beta-Awareness Scale"* [in *"Lesson 1"*] and between "0"-and-"4" on the *"Standard Model"* [illustrated in more detail in *"Lesson 2"*]. But there is more to know about in *Systemology* than is displayed in the graphic models of these previous lessons (booklets).

As we experience it, *"perception"* *does* involve *Awareness*—because it concerns information ("data") that the *Alpha-Spirit* (the individual or actual *Self*) is *"aware of."* In regards to the Human Experience: what we are *"perceiving"* relates to "sensory data" about the environment (usually restricted to *Beta-Existence*)—or about the condition of the *genetic-vehicle* itself. By "sensory data" we mean *sensed* using "physical body" *sensors*.

We differentiate the "Human" range of *perception* in *Systemology*, because it relates to communication-relay between the *"Body"* and *"Mind."* It is only as a result of this *internal "processing"* of sensory perception by the Mind, that the *Alpha-Spirit* is *"aware of"* any Human Experience—what a *genetic-vehicle* is experiencing.

For example: if we speak of the *senses* or *sensation*, we mean the direct "stimulat-

ion" of *sensory receptors* of the physical organism in *Beta-Existence*; whereas *perception* is the assigning of meaning to
sensory data. The *"Body"* transmits sig-
nals to the *"Mind"* for interpretation. This
is the extent that *Self* can be *"aware"*
without *actually* "looking." A *fragmented*
unclear communication on this line results in a difficult experience for *Self*.

The philosopher, Aldous Huxley, men-
tions his own belief about *Self-Honesty* in
his book *"Doors to Perception"* (1954),
titled after the William Blake quote open-
ing this lesson. He refers to it as the
"Mind-at-Large," and cites his academic
inspiration, quoting a Cambridge philosopher, C. D. Broad:

"Each person is at each moment potentially capable of remembering all
that has ever happened to him and of
perceiving everything that is happening everywhere in the universe. The

function of the 'brain' and 'nervous system' is to protect us from being overwhelmed and confused by the mass of largely useless and irrelevant knowledge, by shutting out most of what we should otherwise perceive or remember at any moment, and leaving us only that very small and special selection which is likely to be practically useful. According to such a theory, each one of us is potentially Mind-at-Large."

Later on, Huxley describes his own pinnacle *realization* of what he considers "*egolessness*":

"In the final stage of [*Self-Actualization*], there is an 'obscure knowledge' that All is in all—that All is actually in each. This is as near, I take it, as a finite mind can ever come to 'perceiving everything that is happening everywhere in the Universe.'"

As an applied philosophy, *Systemology* techniques are intended to systematically "clear" or "cleanse" the "lenses" of *perception*. For the *Alpha-Spirit* to achieve any degree of *Self-Honest* "point-of-view" (or "POV") on the Human experience, we systematically examine and "analytically process" various layers and degrees of *fragmented* "thought associations," "reactive-response mechanism" and "emotional turbulence."

THE NATURE OF FRAGMENTATION

We have introduced the nature of the *Alpha-Spirit*, or individual themselves [*in "Lesson 1"*]; and the nature of the *existences* an individual experiences as *reality* [*in "Lesson 2"*]. The next main focus of study is called *fragmentation*. It regards an *Alpha-Spirit's* clarity of *Awareness* and certainty when "perceiving" any *existence*.

True *Knowingness* is an *"Alpha"* quality. It seldom enters into the *Human Condition*, which is "wired" to excessively "figure" and "think." In the absence of *Knowingness* and certainty (at *"Alpha"* levels), we likely experience a network of associative *thought* or *"Thinkingness"* (and *fragmentation*) within the Mind-System.

At an *Alpha* level, when a *Spiritual Being* is "interested" in something, it *knows* by *looking*. If experiencing the *Human Condition* (*Alpha-Spirit* + *genetic-vehicle*), and that "point-of-view" (POV) is extended toward *Beta-Existence*, *Awareness* passes through various systems of *thought* and *feeling* (as represented by the *ZU-Line*).

Our thoughts and emotional turbulence have the ability to affect our *perceptions* — our experience of *reality*. The *ZU-Line* represents a metaphoric "telescopic *lens*" that the *Alpha-Spirit* uses to *perceive* "interior" *Beta* conditions from an "exterior"

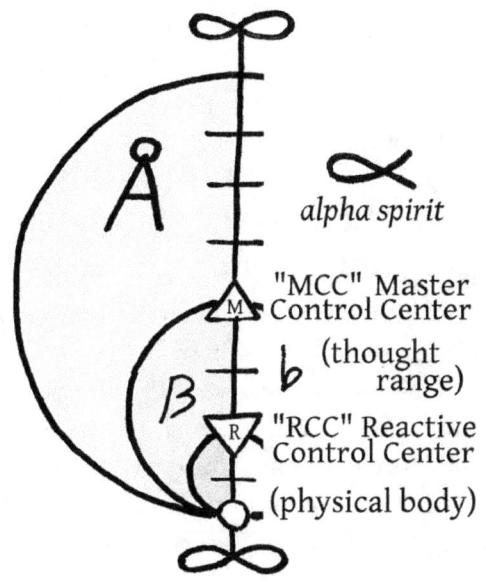

alpha spirit

"MCC" Master Control Center

(thought range)

"RCC" Reactive Control Center

(physical body)

Alpha source-point. It has many layers of potential filtering or *fragmentation*.

One of the primary issues with experiencing *Beta-Existence* using indirect relays of communication, is the *fragmentation* inherent in the Mind-System. It acts as a relay of *perceived* data between the *genetic-vehicle* and the *Alpha-Spirit*. The relay from the *"Mind"* to the *Alpha-Spirit* is at "4" (the "MCC") on the *Standard Model*.

The same message is conveyed to the *Alpha-Spirit* whether *sensed* from an *external* environment in *Beta* or from the *internal* mechanisms of the *"Mind."* The Mind-System does not distinguish between "internal" or "external" sources of *perceptual* information. Determining *"source"* with certainty is a part of *Self-Honesty*.

For example: whether something *sensed* in the external environment is an "actual" presence of danger (or emergency), or whether environmental *facets* are "only"

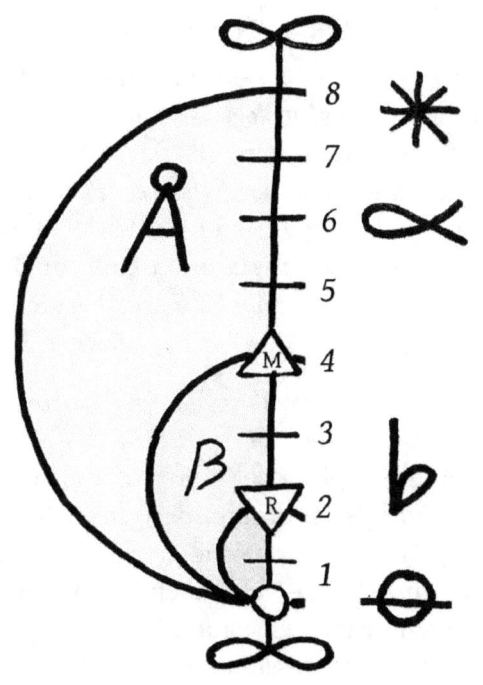

internally *associated* with an idea of danger (due to *fragmented* data from past experience), the same *reality* is *perceived*: that "environment equals dangerous."

The first type of personal *fragmentation* studied in *Systemology* is called "*imprinting*." An "*imprint*" might be best understood as a "*slate*" or "*glass slide*" storing emotional energy from turbulent memories. These *slides* replace, obscure, or distort, the data *perceived* by an *Alpha-Spirit* —and its "clear view" of experience.

To understand better what *imprints* are— or what an "*imprinting incident*" is—consider the typical definition of the word "*imprint*" itself, prompting our choice of using it. It is a "strong impression" or "facsimile image" of something *perceived* as significant. Consider, for example, your "first impressions" of something.

For example: there are many "words" that when spoken seem to have a "trigger" effect on an individual. There is something reactively summoned into view of the *"Mind"* that is then responded to automatically. We refer to this type of information as *"imprinted"* upon the individual. Regardless of what is presented or experienced afterward, the entire "subject" or "concept" will be "filtered" through unclear *imprinted* lenses.

EMOTIONALLY ENCODED IMPRINTS

In addition to the *fragmented* data itself, the personal energy ("ZU") that is "entangled up" in maintaining continuous creation and unknowing storage of *imprints,* also lowers *Awareness.* The "Human Condition" allows *Self* to *perceive reality* using the misinformation continuously fed to it through low-*Awareness* states. Such is the recipe for *hypnotism.*

Thus, "standard-issue" Humans are suspended in a kind of *hypnotic state.*

There are many types of *imprints,* but those that contain the greatest "energy-mass" are the ones that cause the greatest *fragmentation.* In essence they "restrict"—or increase *resistance* against—free-flow of *Spiritual Life Energy* along the *ZU-Line.* They also "restrict" an individual's *Awareness*—and *perception* of *reality*—to rigidly fixed specific considerations rather than having a full-range to choose from and experience.

At an organic level, the cellular and genetic storage of *imprinting* once served an "evolutionary" purpose. Automated response-reaction mechanisms assisted in protecting organic life in the absence of any higher form of reasoning. In the 1960's, those involved in "consciousness expanding" "psychedelic experiments" stumbled onto this phenomenon and began referring to its data as "cellular memory" or "genetic memory."

The *Alpha-Spirit* is also capable of *creating* its own automated-mechanisms of the Mind-System. This happens *knowingly* at first; but, as the circuitry is *validated* and strengthened with increased usage, the "automation" becomes more solid. The individual eventually loses conscious *awareness* of the activity, yet *unknowingly* continues to compulsively *create* these mechanisms with their own *Spiritual Energy* ("ZU").

The Human Condition (the *Alpha-Spirit* + *genetic-vehicle* combination) includes *fragmented* "thought" and "considerations"— but if that were *all* it entailed, it would be a matter of simply "changing our minds" about *reality*, &tc. And the truth is, it *should* be that easy. But another layer of truth reveals that our *considerations* and *beliefs* or *reality-agreements* are actually reinforced quite solidly in *Beta-Existence* as the experience of "emotion."

Unlike "analytical thought" alone, the experience of "emotions" includes a physiological response by the "body" (*genetic-vehicle*). When maintaining a low-order of *Awareness*, such *sensations* actually reinforce (or "*validate*") the *reality* of something—and these are *duplicated* as *reality* in one's own "Personal Universe."

For example: the *Alpha-Spirit* is not actually located in physical space-time or energy-mass bodies of *Beta-Existence*. We experience the Human Condition *remotely* from *outside* this Universe—but we also *create* a *facsimile-duplicate* of the data *perceived* from the Human experience. This is an *Alpha-Spirit's* "Personal Universe." It also includes any data and potential "*mental imagery*" that may be *created* "mentally" at *Will*.

When we consciously (*knowingly*) use our *Awareness* to *create* "*mental imagery*" (or confront any data) in the "*Mind,*" we *realize* our "ownership" of the *creation* and have the ability to also "*uncreate*" it at *Will*. But, in the case of "*imprints*" (*fragmentation*), an experience of the "*imagery*" and its *triggered* emotional response is *unknowingly created*. Energy is compulsively suspended or entangled in maintaining its continual *creation*.

That which we are *freely* able to "consider" (or *create*) does not generally give us much trouble. But then, most of what we would choose to *create* is desirable or interesting, if not pleasurable. The contents of an *imprint* are usually things we *don't* want to "confront"—thus, we will not *perceive* or "see" a thing "*As-It-Is.*"

Imprints are very much like "snapshots" of *perceived reality*. The experience of them as a "*mental image*" is not restricted only

to "visual" scenery. *Imprints* include a record of all *facets* experienced in the *"imprinting incident."* By *facets*, we mean *all*
data—yes, visual, but also, sound, smell,
lighting, time of day, temperature, hu-
midity, objects present, persons present,
body positions, motions... All of this is recorded *and* associated.

The type of *"imagery"* (or content) that we
are reactively unable or unwilling to *confront* (*"As-It-Is"*) is generally *considered*
"dangerous" or "painful" or similar.
Whatever it is, it is *perceived* to threaten
optimum survival conditions—reinforced
and inflated by an *emotional* "charge" and
physiological ("body") response. This
prompts "unpleasant" *feelings* when *con-
fronted* with any *facet* previously *imprinted*
as "unpleasant."

Yet, what we are unable to *confront* is
what we are constantly being faced with
or chased by. Data from the *imprinting in-*

cident is continuously created and stored (and automatically retrieved) as part of our defense-mechanisms to help us avoid danger and pain. This once seemed like a good thing. But since this occurs automatically and obscures a clear view, it is *fragmentation*—inhibiting one's free considerations of thought.

CHANNELS AND CIRCUITS

In *Systemology*, the *ZU-Line* of the *Standard Model* is a theoretical construct or graphic representation of the *Alpha-Spirit* as a unit of *Awareness*. It is, in itself, the primary "channel" of communication—or energy-flow—that is directed by the *Alpha-Spirit* as an *Awareness*; otherwise considered the "perspective" from *Self*.

As an *Awareness*, our "intended" focus on some "*thing*" establishes a present-time "channel" of communication (and energy) that is best defined as *"attention."* Essentially, anything that we have our *"attention"* on, we are making "contact" with using a focused "energy beam" of our *Awareness.*

When we refer to a *thing,* we generally mean its *form* and *substance* as a "mass" or construct. We also share an *"affinity"* with all *things*—either an impulse toward or a repulsion from; an emotional response of some kind. Because any *thing* (even as a concept) is a potential contact point for our "channel" of communication (and *attention-energy*), we refer to any *form, object* or *person* as a "terminal" in our *Systemology* vocabulary.

The relationship we have with any *terminal* will be evident by the quality of *channel* that is experienced. In most cases, the nature of the "energy-flow" will be determined by previous experiences and/or *reality-agreements*. The idea that we "learn" from "experience" and store data as "memory" is not a new concept. The way in which it occurs and how it affects our *perceptions* is, however, rarely explored systematically.

Early in the existence of a personal "*Spiritual Timeline*," the *Alpha-Spirit* starts out very much like a "clean slate"—engaging in *creation* and *existence* as a "being" with practically unlimited power and range of willingness to experience. We were once willing to extend "*attention*"—and therefore "reach"—anywhere.

As *fragmentation* accumulates (and *Actualized Awareness* declines), an individual is less likely to *be*, *know* about, *think* of, *act* toward or *own* various "things." This is, again, evident in the quality of the "channel" maintained with any representative *terminal*. If turbulent, there is likely an *imprint* strongly influencing it. As *Aware-*

ness declines, a being is willing to engage with fewer *terminals* and "reach" less into *existence.*

Fragmentation is not only composed of "emotional encoding." Even when it is, there are many factors that can make it seem quite "rational." Sometimes a *fragmented channel* is simply "cluttered with debris." It may concern what first appears like "factual data"—but is misaligned, misappropriated or just false altogether. Thus, *"defragmentation"* concerns "clearing the debris" (or "energy blocks") from *channels* to any *terminal.*

In *Systemology*, we recognize that a *channel* consists of three primary "circuits" that we use to *perceive* an experience with any *terminal.* These *circuits* are distinguished by the flow-type of *attention-energy* an *Alpha-Spirit* employs. For example: the first *circuit* is an "out-flow" of energy—meaning our experiences when "extending" or "reaching toward" a *terminal*; what *we* have done *to* or *about* some *terminal*.

The second *circuit* is the "in-flow" of energy we receive from the environment or *terminal*—or else what the *terminal* has done *to* or *about us*. And finally, the third *circuit* concerns "cross-flows" of energy that we are able to observe, which means what *others* have done *about* or *to* the *terminal*. As a form of "social" learning, this also includes what we have "overheard" others "communicating"to others about the *terminal* as well.

Data from these three *circuits* affects the general overall quality of the *channel* we use to experience *reality* regarding a certain *terminal*. Much like the *"emotionally encoded imprints,"* the information and *facets* stored from direct experience or observation can easily serve as a "filter" that screens present-time experiences. In other words, it *unknowingly* affects what we are "reaching" and "withdrawing" from in our everyday *life*.

The solution toward freeing up the original stores of energy we possess—and therefore widening our range for thought-consideration and experience—is quite similar to the philosophy behind other *Systemology techniques*. A *Seeker* examines their *unknowing* ("*not-known*") participation with, and agreements about, *reality* at an accessible "above-the-surface" level of *Knowingness* (and *Self-Determinism*). The act of *living deliberately* is a practiced skill in this world.

LEVELS OF ACTUALIZED REALIZATION

Systemology does not ignore a healthy use of what most consider "*intuition*"—or else *actual* high-level *Knowingness*. Of course, many individuals misappropriate or misinterpret "*intuition*" with being the same as "how they *feel*"—and these are not the same thing.

True *intuition* is not a "conditioned" or "programmed" *Knowingness*; it comes from "higher faculties" and not "lower" *emotional responses* which may be easily misaligned with a few painful experiences—or even one big one. True *intuition* is unlocked by increasing our levels of *actualized realization* and *clear perception*.

Self-Actualizing the first level of understanding means being able to affirm in *Self-Honesty*: "*I act as I will.*" This does not mean "doing whatever" without regard to consequence. On the contrary, a *Self-Actualized* individual, free of *fragmentation*, is able to make the best possible decisions in regards to *Life*. The *Seeker* is

69

regaining control—no longer allowing the *genetic-vehicle* to simply run itself solely on "stimulus-response."

This first level concerns control of physical behaviors of a *genetic-vehicle*—primarily by maintaining *Self*-control of "emotional states" in *Self-Honesty*. Only then can we actually be *Self-determined* in our actions—and, of course, clear in our "efforts" on a physical level. This is practiced in basic *Systemology* exercises.

The second level of *Actualized Awareness* concerns the Mind-System directly: a *Self-Honest* handling of "thought"—the realized freedom and ability to "*Think as I will.*" We mean literally, the ability to "think clearly" and consider a full range of thoughts without inhibition or negative emotional responses. In *Systemology Processing*, we work toward this level of *Awareness* with "*Beta-Defragmentation*" techniques.

Higher levels of *Awareness* extend beyond the Mind-System and pertain to the *Alpha-Spirit* as a *Beingness*. A third level of potential *Awareness* concerns *"Creating as I will"* in an *"Alpha-Existence."* Beyond this, we stand at the *Gateways of Infinity* and can confirm *"I am as I will."* Studies and techniques focused on these higher levels are treated in *Systemology Processing* as *"Alpha-Defragmentation."*

Collectively, this systematic journey towards a "higher" and more ideal "spiritual" state of *Awareness* is referred to as *"The Pathway."* An understanding of this *"Pathway"* may be earned by studying our philosophy and applying its techniques. While this *Basic Course* series is intended to provide the principle *"Fundamentals"* that all *Systemologists* should know, there is still much ground ahead for a *Seeker* to explore.

PRACTICE EXERCISES

1. Look around the room. Spot an
   object that you like. Focus your
   attention solely on the object and
   nothing else; nothing else in the
   environment and no internal
   activity of the Mind. Do your best
   to simply *be* with the object, but
   also committing its "form" to
   memory—without analyzing any
   reactions or other thought associations. Now, close your eyes and
   "mentally" *imagine* a copy (or facsimile) of the object—*imagining* its
   details as closely resembling the
   "original" as possible. Dissolve it,
   collapse it, or throw it away—
   then make another copy. Do this
   several times until you are satis-

fied with the appearance of the copy and the *Awareness* that you are knowingly creating the *mental image*. Then, intend for this copy to be "brighter" than before, and see it appear as such; then "dimmer." Practice this alternation a few times. Now, intend for its apparent color to change: make it "blue"; change it to "red"; turn it "green"; then finally return it to its original color. Dissolve this image and then open your eyes. Record any *realizations* you may have had in your journal.

2. Recall a time something seemed *real* to you. [It could be an object, a place, a person, or an event (or situation) that contains any of these—which considered *facets* of the incident.] Take a moment to notice details about the *mental imagery* that is "called to Mind." Are

there parts that immediately come into view? Are there parts you have to try hard to *imagine* or "fill in"? Practice this with various "things" (*terminals*). After spending some time with this, select one of the times recalled, then recreate it, but *intentionally* changing some of the data viewed. You might change the color of an object, or replace a person present with another individual, *&tc.* — whatever it takes to demonstrate your ability to *knowingly alter* the recalled data.

3. Get the sense of making the "body" sit (or lie down). Focus all your *Awareness* (*attention*) on just the feet, without considering the remainder of the legs or the rest of the body. If this proves too broad of a scope at first, focus on just one toe of one foot. While

concentrating *Awareness* in that location, *imagine* the feet as nonexistent—or else, *consider* that if the feet *were* nonexistent, then *Self* would still continue its (*Alpha*) existence, unchanged, as an *Alpha-Spirit*. Then, *consider* that feet are useful for moving the "body" (*genetic-vehicle*) across "space" (in *Beta-Existence*), but that they are *not* the actual "feet" of the *Alpha-Spirit*; and the true *Self* is in no way dependent on physical "feet" in order to "act." It is important for an *Alpha-Spirit* to be in "good communication" with the *genetic-vehicle* to get along well in *Beta-Existence*, but it should in no way confuse its own *identity* with that of a *body*.

4. Refer to the previous exercise. Continue focusing *Awareness* on the other remaining points of the

"body"—the legs, pelvic region, stomach, chest, arms, hands, neck, and head. Treat each point with the same *considerations*—and move off from each with the same *realizations*—as with the feet. When these points have all been spotted, the *Seeker* may *consider* the whole body of the *genetic-vehicle* as a useful instrument for communication and activity in the *Physical Universe*. It is biologically adapted for organic life in *Beta-Existence*—but *Self*, the "I-AM" or *Alpha-Spirit, is* above and superior to, independent and apart from, the *genetic-vehicle*. The ideal "end-point" of this exercise is to get a sense of *Self* actually operating from a *Spiritual "Alpha"* point of *Beingness, exterior* to a *genetic-vehicle* and *Beta-Existence* altogether; but this *realization* cannot be forced prematurely.

5. Make two lists of significant "*terminals*" in your life: "things" you like very much; and "things" you don't like at all. Remember: "*terminals*" are "things" consisting of "mass"—persons, places, objects, *&tc.* Use several sheets/pages as needed, but keep the two lists separated. Of course there are many things encountered in *Life*, but we are interested in the most significant ones that readily "come to mind." When the lists are satisfactorily completed, take each "item" listed and "scan" your surface memory for instances or occurrences that involved that *terminal.* Alternate between the two lists to avoid excessively focusing on the "negatives." See if you can get a sense or idea of *why* you "feel" a certain way about a particular "item." It

may help to refer to the section on "Channels and Circuits" to target specific "types" of energy-flow that pertain to a *terminal*. If you find that "thinking about" an incident involving a "thing you don't like" is causing you major discomfort: alternate *spotting* something in the incident and *spotting* something in the room (or environment) until its handled.

6. Using your lists from the previous exercise: take each listed "item" and *practice* intending your "feelings" about that particular *terminal* to change to the opposing list. Once you have a sense of it, intend your "feelings" to switch back to how they were. Practice alternating your "feelings" in this fashion. It may be easier to treat items you are more

"neutral" on at first. The exercise is simply a demonstration of how the control of such *considerations* ultimately rests with our *Self*. Obviously the goal is not to get a *Seeker* to dislike things they like, but to establish just how "fluid" our feelings actually are. Ideally, we would like to see, at the very least, a "softening" of the harsher emotional responses that "things we don't like" seem to inspire in us. It does not mean we have to "like" such things or engage with them; but, we want to reach an acceptable tolerance level that enables us to *confront* (or "face up to") their *reality*—to be at "*cause*" over their handling and how they are duplicated (or "copied") in our Personal Universe, rather than reactively withdraw and unwillingly (or *unknowingly*) remain an "*effect*."

79

7. Seat the "body" comfortably in a quiet room. With eyes closed, "mentally" (*intentionally*) "reach" out with your *Awareness* and hold all of your *attention* on the two rear "upper-corners" of the room (the corners *behind* where the body is located). *Intend* to focus all of your present-time "*interest*" on only these "corners" and think of nothing else. That is the totality of the exercise. If other "thoughts" invade your *Awareness*, simply return all of your "*interest*" on the "corners." Hold this *intention* for as long as you can, working up to handling longer durations of time with practice. An hour or more of actual practice is effectively more beneficial than any other known traditional "meditation" technique. "Corners" of a room are

"points" that define the "*space.*" A room has eight of these "anchor points" in all. This exercise may be extended to gradually increase the number of "corners" that you can hold your *attention* on simultaneously.

Continue learning
The Fundamentals of Systemology
in your next
Basic Course
lesson booklet:

ANCIENT SYSTEMOLOGY:
WISDOM OF THE ARCANE TABLETS

GLOSSARY

actualization : to make actual, not just potential; to bring into full solid Reality; to realize fully in *Awareness* as a "thing."

agreement (reality) : unanimity of opinion of what is "thought" to be known; an accepted arrangement of how things are; things we consider as "real" or as an "is" of "reality"; a consensus of what is real as made by standard-issue (common) participants; what an individual contributes to or accepts as "real"; in *Systemology*, a synonym for *"reality."*

alpha : the first, primary, basic, superior or beginning of some form; in *Systemology*, referring to the state of existence operating on spiritual archetypes and postulates, will and intention "exterior" to the low-level condensation and solidarity of energy and matter as the 'physical universe'.

alpha-spirit : a "spiritual" *Life*-form; the "true" *Self* or I-AM; the *individual*; the spiritual (*alpha*) *Self* that is animating the (*beta*) physical body or "*genetic vehicle*" using a continuous *Lifeline* of spiritual ("*ZU*") energy; an individual spiritual (*alpha*) entity possessing no physical mass or measurable waveform (motion) in the Physical Universe as itself, so it animates the (*beta*) physical body or "*genetic vehicle*" as a catalyst to experience *Self*-determined causality in effect within the *Physical Universe*; a singular unit or point of *Spiritual Awareness* that is *Aware* that it is *Aware*.

alpha thought : the highest spiritual *Self-determination* over creation and existence exercised by an Alpha-Spirit; the Alpha range of pure *Creative Ability* based on direct postulates and considerations of *Beingness*; spiritual qualities comparable to "thought" but originating in Alpha-existence (at "6.0") independently superior to a *beta-anchored* Mind-System, although an Alpha-Spirit may use Will ("5.0") to carry the intentions of a postulate or consideration ("6.0") to the Master Control Center ("4.0").

ascension : actualized *Awareness* elevated to the point of true "spiritual existence" exterior to *beta existence*. An "Ascended Master" is one who has returned to an incarnation on Earth as an inherently *Enlightened One*, demonstrable in their actions—they have the ability to *Self-direct* the "Spirit" as *Self* and maintain consciousness beyond this existence as a personal identity continuum with the same *Self-directed* control and communication of Will-Intention that is exercised, actualized and developed deliberately during one's present incarnation.

associative knowledge : significance or meaning of a facet or aspect assigned to (or considered to have) a direct relationship with another facet; to connect or relate ideas or facets of existence with one another; a reactive-response image, emotion or conception that is suggested by (or directly accompanies) something other than itself; in traditional systems logic, an equivalency of significance or meaning between facets or sets that are grouped together, such as in $(a + b) + c = a + (b + c)$; in NexGen Systemology, erroneous associative knowledge is assignment of the same value to all facets or parts considered as related (even when they are not actually so), such as in $a = a, b = a, c = a$ and so forth without distinction.

attention : active use of *Awareness* toward a specific aspect or thing; the act of "attending" with the presence of *Self*; a direction of focus or concentration of *Awareness* along a particular channel or conduit or toward a particular terminal node or communication termination point; the Self-directed concentration of personal energy as a combination of observation, thought-waves and consideration; focused application of *Self-Directed Awareness*.

awareness : the highest sense of-and-as Self in knowing and being as I-AM (the *Alpha-Spirit*); the extent of beingness directed as a POV experienced by Self as knowingness.

beta (awareness) : all consciousness activity ("*Awareness*") in the "Physical Universe" (KI) or else *beta-existence*; *Awareness* within the range of the *genetic-body*, including material thoughts, emotional responses and physical motors; personal *Awareness* of physical energy and physical matter moving through physical space and experienced as "time"; the *Awareness* held by *Self* that is restricted to a physical organic *Lifeform* or "*genetic vehicle*" in which it experiences causality in the *Physical Universe*.

beta (existence) : all manifestation in the "Physical Universe" (KI); the "Physical" state of existence consisting of vibrations of physical energy and physical matter moving through physical space and experienced as "time"; the conditions of *Awareness* for the *Alpha-spirit* (*Self*) as a physical organic *Lifeform* or "*genetic vehicle*" in which it experiences causality in the *Physical Universe*.

beta-defragmentation : toward a state of *Self-Honesty* in regards to handling experience of the "Physical Universe" (*beta-existence*); an applied spiritual philosophy (or technology) of Self-Actualization

channel : a specific stream, course, current, direction or route; to form or cut a groove or ridge or otherwise guide along a specific course; a direct path; an artificial aqueduct created to connect two water bodies or water or make travel possible.

circuit : a circular path or loop; a closed-path within a system that allows a flow; a pattern or action or wave movement that follows a specific route or potential path only.

condense (condensation) : the transition of vapor to liquid; denoting a change in state to a more substantial or solid condition; leading to a more compact or solid form.

consideration : careful analytical reflection of all aspects; deliberation; determining the significance of a "thing" in relation to similarity or dissimilarity to other "things"; evaluation of facts and importance of certain facts; thorough examination of all aspects related to, or important for, making a decision; the analysis of consequences and estimation of significance when making decisions.

continuity : being a continuous whole; a complete whole or "total round of"; the balance of the equation ["–120" + "120" = "0" &*tc.*]; an apparent unbroken interconnected coherent whole; also, as applied to Universes in *Systemology*, the lowest base consideration of space-time or commonly shared level of energy-matter apparent in an existence, or else the lowest degree of solidity or condensation whereby all mass that exists is identifiable or communicable with all other mass that exists; represented as "0" on the *Standard Model* for the Physical Universe (*beta-existence*), a level of existence that is below Human emotion, comparable to the solidity of "rocks" and "walls" and "inert bodies."

defragmentation : the *reparation* of wholeness; collecting all dispersed parts to reform an original whole; a process of removing "*fragmentation*" in data or knowledge to provide a clear understanding; applying techniques and processes that promote a *holistic* interconnected *alpha* state, favoring observational *Awareness* of continuity in all spiritual and physical systems; in *Systemology*, a "*Seeker*" achieving an actualized state of basic "*Self-Honest Awareness*" is said to have completed *beta-defragmentation*, whereas *Alpha-defragmentation* is the rehabilitation of the *creative ability*, managing the *Spiri-*

tual Timeline and the POV of *Self* as Alpha-Spirit (I-AM).

existence : the *state* or fact of *apparent manifestation*; the resulting combination of the Principles of Manifestation: consciousness, motion and substance; continued *survival*; that which independently exists.

exterior : outside of; on the outside; in *Systemology*, we mean specifically the POV of *Self* that is *'outside of'* the *Human Condition,* free of the physical and mental trappings of the Physical Universe; a metahuman range of consideration; see also '*Zu-Vision*'.

external : a force coming from outside; information received from outside sources; in *Systemology*, the objective *'Physical Universe'* existence, or *beta-existence*, that the Physical Body or *genetic vehicle* is essentially *anchored* to for its considerations of locational space-time as a dimension or POV.

facets : an aspect, an apparent phase; one of many faces of something; a cut surface on a gem or crystal; in *Systemology*—a single perception or aspect of a memory or "*Imprint*"; any one of many ways in which a memory is recorded; perceptions associated with a painful emotional (sensation) experience and "*imprinted*" onto a metaphoric lens through which to view future similar experiences; other secondary terminals that are associated with a particular terminal, painful event or experience of loss, and which may exhibit the same encoded significance as the activating event.

feedback loop : a complete and continuous circuit flow of energy or information directed as an output from a source to a target which is altered and return back to the source as an input; in *General Systemology*—the continuous process where outputs of a system are routed back as inputs to complete a circuit or loop, which may be closed or connected to other systems/circuits; in *Systemology*—the continuous process where directed *Life* energy and *Awareness* is sent back to *Self* as experience, understanding and memory to complete an energetic circuit as a loop.

fragmentation : breaking into parts and scattering the pieces; the *fractioning* of wholeness or the *fracture* of a holistic interconnected *alpha* state, favoring observational *Awareness* of perceived connectivity between parts; *discontinuity*; separation of a totality into parts; in *Systemology*, a person outside a state of *Self-Honesty* is said to be *fragmented*.

genetic-vehicle : a physical *Life*-form; the physical (*beta*) body that is animated/controlled by the (*Alpha*) *Spirit* using a continuous *Lifeline* (ZU); a physical (*beta*) organic receptacle and catalyst for the (*Alpha*) *Self* to operate "causes" and experience "effects" within the *Physical Universe*.

gradient : a degree of partitioned ascent or descent along some scale, elevation or incline; "higher" and "lower" values in relation to one another.

holistic : the examination of interconnected systems as encompassing something greater than the *sum* of their "parts."

imagination : the ability to create *mental imagery* in one's Personal Universe at will and change or alter it as desired; the ability to create, change and dissolve mental images on command or as an act of will; to create a mental image or have associated imagery displayed (or "conjured") in the mind that may or may not be treated as real (or memory recall) and may or may not accurately duplicate objective reality; to employ *creative abilities* of the Spirit that are independent of reality agreements with beta-existence.

intention : directed application of Will; to intend (have "in Mind") or signify (give "significance" to) for or toward a particular purpose; in *Systemology* (from the *Standard Model*)—the spiritual activity at WILL (5.0) directed by an *Alpha Spirit* (7.0); the application of WILL as "Cause" from a higher order of Alpha Thought and consideration (6.0).

interior : inside of; on the inside; in *Systemology*, we mean specifically the POV of *Self* that is fixed to the *'internal' Human Condition,* including the *Reactive Control Center* (RCC) and Mind-System or *Master Control Center* (MCC); within *beta-existence*.

internal : a force coming from inside; information received from inside sources; in *Systemology*, the objective experience of *beta-existence* associated with the Physical Body or *genetic vehicle* and its POV regarding sensation and perception; from inside the body; in the body.

Human Condition : a standard default state of Human experience, generally accepted to be the extent of its potential identity (*beingness*).

imprint : to strongly impress, stamp, mark (or outline) onto a softer 'impressible' substance; to mark with pressure onto a surface; in *Systemology*, used to indicate permanent Reality impressions marked by frequencies, energies or interactions experienced during periods of emotional distress, pain, unconsciousness, loss, enforcement, or something antagonistic to physical (personal) survival, all of which are are stored with other reactive response-mechanisms at lower-levels of *Awareness* as opposed to the active memory database and proactive processing center of the Mind; an experiential "memory-set" that may later resurface—be triggered or stimulated artificially—as Reality, of which similar responses will be engaged automatically; holographic-like imagery "stamped" onto consciousness as composed of energetic *facets* tied to the "snap-shot" of an experience.

imprinting incident : the first or original event instance communicated and *emotionally encoded* onto an individual's "*Spiritual Timeline*" (recorded memory from all lifetimes), which formed a permanent impression that is later used to mechanistically treat future contact on that channel; the first or original occurrence of some particular *facet* or mental image related to a certain type of *encoded response*, such as pain and discomfort, losses and victimization, and even the acts that we have taken against others along the *Spiritual Timeline* of our existence that caused them to also be *Imprinted*.

knowledge : clear personal processing of informed understanding; information (data) that is actualized as effectively workable understanding; a demonstrable understanding on which we may 'set' our *Awareness*—or literally a "knowledge."

Master-Control-Center (MCC) : a perfect computing device to the extent of the information received from "lower levels" of sensory experience/perception; the proactive communication system of the "*Mind*"; a relay point of active *Awareness* along the Identity's *ZU-line*, which is responsible for maintaining basic *Self-Honest* clarity of *Knowingness* as a *seat of consciousness* between the *Alpha-Spirit* and the secondary "*Reactive Control Center*" of a *Life-form* in *beta existence*; the Mind-center for an *Alpha-Spirit* to actualize cause in the *beta existence*; the analytical *Self-Determined* Mind-center of an *Alpha-Spirit used* to project *Will* toward the genetic body; the point of contact between *Spiritual Systems* and the *beta existence*; presumably the "*Third Eye*" of a being connected directly to the *I-AM-Self*, which is responsible for *determining* Reality at any time; in *Systemology*, this is plotted at (4.0) on the continuity model of the *ZU-line*.

mental image : a subjectively experienced "picture" created and imagined into being by the Alpha-Spirit (or at lower levels, one of its automated mechanisms) that includes all perceptible *facets* of totally immersive scene, which may be forms originated by an individual, or a "facsimile-copy" ("snap-shot") of something seen or encountered; a duplication of wave-forms in one's Personal Universe as a "picture" that mirror an "external" Universe experience, such as an *Imprint*.

perception : internalized processing of data received by the *senses*; to become *Aware of* via the senses.

point-of-view (POV) : a point to view from; an opinion or attitude as expressed from a specific identity-phase; a specific standpoint or vantage-point; a definitive manner of consideration specific to an individual phase or identity; a place or position affording a specific view or vantage; circumstances and programming of an individual that is conducive to a particular response, consideration or belief-set (paradigm); a position (consideration) or place (location) that provides a specific view or perspective (subjective) on experience (of the objective). May also be referred to in our texts as a "*viewpoint.*"

processing, systematic : the inner-workings or "through-put" result of systems; in *Systemology*, a methodology of applied spiritual technology used toward personal Self-Actualization; methods of selective directed attention, communicated language and associative imagery that targets an increase in personal control of the human condition.

reactive control center (RCC) : the secondary (reactive) communication system of the "*Mind*"; a relay point of *Awareness* along the Identity's *ZU-line*, which is responsible for engaging basic motors, biochemical processes and any *programmed automated responses* of a living *beta* organism; the reactive Mind-Center of a living organism relaying communications of *Awareness* between causal experience of *Physical Systems* and the "*Master Control Center*"; it presumably stores all emotional encoded imprints as fragmentation of *ZU* (within the range of the "*psychological/ emotive systems*" of a being), which it may *react* to as Reality at any time; in *Systemology*, this is plotted at (2.0) on the continuity model of the *ZU-line*.

reality : see "*agreement.*"

Seeker : an individual on the *Pathway to Self-Honesty*; a practitioner of *Mardukite Systemology* or *Systemology Processing* that is working toward *Spiritual Ascension*.

Self-actualization : bringing the full potential of the Human spirit into Reality; expressing full capabilities and creativeness of the *Alpha-Spirit*.

Self-determinism : the freedom to act, clear of external control or influence; the personal control of Will to direct intention.

Self-honesty : the basic or original *alpha* state of *being* and *knowing*; clear and present total *Awareness* of-and-as *Self*, in its most basic and true proactive expression of itself as *Spirit* or *I-AM*—free of artificial attachments, perceptive filters and other emotionally-reactive or mentally-conditioned programming imposed on the human condition by the systematized physical world; the ability to experience existence without judgment.

sensation : an external stimulus received by internal sense organs (receptors/sensors); sense impressions.

slate : a hard thin flat surface material used for writing on; a chalk-board, which is a large version of the original wood-framed writing slate, named for the rock-type it was made from.

Spheres of Existence (dynamic systems) : a model of *eight* concentric circles, rings or spheres (each larger than the former) that is overlaid onto the Standard Model of Beta-Existence to demonstrate dynamic systems of existence extending out from a POV of Self (often as a "body") at the *First Sphere*; these are given as a basic eightfold system: *Self, Home/Family, Groups, Humanity, Life on Earth, Physical Universe, Spiritual Universe* and *Infinity-Divinity.*

spiritual timeline : a continuous stream of moment-to-moment *Mental Images* (or a record of experiences) that defines the "past" of a spiritual being (or *Alpha-Spirit*) and which includes impressions (*imprints, &tc.*) form all life-incarnations and significant spiritual events the being has encountered.

Standard Model, The (systemology) : our existential and cosmological *standard model* or cabbalistic model; a "*monistic continuity model*" demonstrating *total system* interconnectivity "above" and "below" observation of any apparent *parameters*; the original presentation of the *ZU-line*, represented as a singular vertical (y-axis) waveform in space across dimensional levels or Universes (*Spheres of Existence*) without charting any specific movement across a dimensional time-graph x-axis; The Standard Model of Systemology represents the basic workable synthesis of common denominators in models explored throughout Grade-I and Grade-II material.

system : from the Greek, "to set together"; to set or arrange things or data together so as to form an orderly understanding of a "whole."

terminal (node) : a point, end or mass on a line; a point or connection for closing an electric circuit, such as a post on a battery terminating at each end of its own systematic function; any end point or 'termination' on a line; a point of connectivity with other points; in systems, any point which may be treated as a contact point of interaction; anything that may be distinguished as an 'is' and is therefore a 'termination point' of a system or along a flow-line which may interact with other related systems it shares a line with; a point of interaction with other points.

thought-form : apparent *manifestation* or existential *realization* of *Thought-waves* as "solids" even when only apparent in Reality-agreements of the Observer; the treatment of *Thought-waves* as permanent *imprints* obscuring *Self-Honest* clarity of *Awareness* when reinforced by emotional experience as actualized "thought-formed solids" ("*beliefs*") in the Mind; energetic patterns that "surround" the individual.

ZU : the ancient Sumerian cuneiform sign for the archaic verb—"*to know,*" "*knowingness*" or "*awareness*"; in *Mardukite Zuism and Systemology*, the active energy/matter of the "Spiritual Universe" (AN) experienced as a *Lifeforce* or *consciousness* that imbues living forms extant in the "Physical Universe" (KI); "*Spiritual Life Energy*"; energy demonstrated by the WILL of an actualized *Alpha-Spirit* in the "Spiritual Universe" (AN), which impinges its *Awareness* into the Physical Universe (KI), animating/controlling *Life* for its experience of *beta-existence* along an individual Alpha-Spirit's personal *Identity-continuum*, called a *ZU-line*.

Zu-Line : a theoretical construct in *Mardukite Zuism and Systemology* demonstrating *Spiritual Life Energy (ZU)* as a personal individual "continuum" of Awareness interacting with all Spheres of Existence on the Standard Model of Systemology; a spectrum of potential variations and interactions of a monistic continuum or singular *Spiritual Life Energy (ZU)* demonstrated on the Standard Model; an energetic channel of potential POV and "locations" of Beingness, demonstrated in early Systemology materials as an individual Alpha-Spirit's personal *Identity-continuum*, potentially connecting *Awareness (ZU)* of *Self* with "*Infinity*" simultaneous with all points considered in existence; a symbolic demonstration of the "*Life-line*" on which *Awareness (ZU)* extends from the direction of the "Spiritual Universe" (AN) in its true original *alpha state* through an entire possible range of activity resulting in its *beta state* and control of a *genetic-entity* occupying the *Physical Universe (KI)*.

THE SYSTEMOL

Seekers and students of the *Basic Course* and *Professional Course* will also be interested in the *Advanced Series* of the *Systemology Core.* These volumes are a complete chronological record of the Mardukite New Thought developments from the Systemology Society, published in 2019 through 2023.

The *Systemology Core* begins with the first professional publication released when the *Mardukite Systemology Society* emerged from the underground in 2019, with: *"The Tablets of Destiny Revelation."*

OGY PATHWAY

The Tablets of Destiny Revelation:
*How Long-Lost Anunnaki Wisdom
Can Change the Fate of Humanity*

Crystal Clear: *Handbook for Seekers*

Metahuman Destinations (*2 volumes*)

Imaginomicon:
Approaching Gateways to Higher Universes

Way of the Wizard: *Utilitarian Systemology*

Systemology-180: *Fast-Track to Ascension*

Systemology Backtrack:
Reclaiming Spiritual Power & Past-Life Memory

PUBLISHED BY THE **JOSHUA FREE** IMPRINT REPRESENTING

The Mardukite Academy of Systemology

THE JOSHUA FREE IMPRINT
JFI PUBLICATIONS

MARDUKITE
ZUISM

mardukite.com

www.ingramcontent.com/pod-product-compliance
Lightning Source LLC
Chambersburg PA
CBHW071208120626
46546CB00006B/2468